MY FIRST COOKERY BOOK

by
Wayne Jackman

illustrated by
Tizzie Knowles

MY FIRST COOKERY BOOK

First published in 1990 by
Firefly Books Limited
61 Western Road, Hove
East Sussex BN3 1JD

© Copyright 1990 Firefly Books Limited

**British Library Cataloguing in
Publication Data**
Jackman, Wayne
  My first cookery book.
  1. Food – Recipes
  I. Title II. Knowles, Tizzie
  641.5

  ISBN 1 85485 0504

Typeset by Nicola Taylor, Wayland
Printed in Italy by G. Canale & C.S.p.A., Turin
Bound in Belgium by Casterman, S.A.

Contents

Introduction

Here are some simple and delicious recipes that are great fun to make. You can do most of them on your own, but sometimes a grown-up will need to help you, especially with the oven. When you have got used to cooking, try to think of your own ways to make the recipes even tastier. Invent your own recipes too!

Remember that kitchen tools can be dangerous if you don't use them properly. Before you start, here are some useful tips about cooking:

- Wash your hands and wipe the working surfaces with a clean cloth.

- Wear an apron and tie back your hair if it is long.

- Read the recipe carefully.

- Collect everything you need and have it ready.

- Wash all fresh fruit and vegetables.

- Wear oven gloves before you touch hot trays.

- Tidy up as you go along, and wash up when you have finished.

Happy cooking!

1 Breakfasts

A good breakfast is the best way to start the day. It will give you bags of energy to work and play. Here are some recipes to brighten up breakfast time.

Billy the Kid Breakfast

This is a breakfast for cowboys and girls,
just right to fill your tummy before
rounding up the cattle.

You will need:

1 large tin of baked beans
1 small tin of frankfurters
1 teaspoon of runny honey
1 pinch of pepper
1 teaspoon of Worcester sauce
or brown sauce
1 pinch of salt

What to do:

Open the tins of beans and frankfurters with a tin opener.
Cut up the frankfurters and put them into a large bowl.
Pour on the beans, honey, sauce, pepper and salt,
and mix it all up.
This will be enough to feed
four hungry cowboys and girls!

Sweet and Spicy Toast

This is a delicious way to eat toast.
Brown bread makes it even tastier.

You will need:

2 slices of bread
Butter or margarine
Honey
Cinnamon

What to do:

Toast the bread (ask a grown-up to help).
Using a knife, spread on the butter or margarine.
Spread honey on the toast.
Sprinkle a pinch of cinnamon
over the honey.

Be careful. The honey might melt a bit and drip off the edge!

Mountain Munch Muesli

In Switzerland people have eaten muesli for hundreds of years. Now it is popular everywhere because it is so good for you. Most supermarkets and health food shops sell the things you need.

You will need:

1 cup of wholewheat flakes
1 cup of rye flakes
1 cup of porridge oats
1 cup of bran flakes
1½ cups of mixed nuts
2 cups of mixed dried fruit
1 cup of raisins

What to do:

Put everything in a large bowl and mix it all together with a wooden spoon.
Put the mixture into an airtight container or plastic bag.
At breakfast time put two or three tablespoons for each person in a bowl.
Add milk. You could try yoghurt or fruit juice instead.

Try different nuts and fruit each time you make a new batch of muesli.

2 Lunchboxes and Picnics

Do you take a lunchbox to school? Do you ever go on picnics? This part of the book tells you how to make some simple, tasty snacks to take with you. Try ideas of your own, especially in the sandwiches.

French Stick Sandwich

You will need:

1 small stick of french bread
Butter or margarine
2 tablespoons of cream cheese or cottage cheese
2 sliced tomatoes
Lettuce leaves
6 slices of salami or sausage
1 tablespoon of chopped
spring onions or chives

What to do:

Slice the bread in half lengthwise (ask a grown-up to help).
Spread each half with butter or margarine.
Spread on the cheese.
Sprinkle on the spring onions
or chives.
Lay slices of salami or
sausage on the cheese.
Add the lettuce and
sliced tomatoes.
Put the two halves together
and cut it in half.

This will make a jumbo meal – big enough for two people!

11

Summer Spread

It's great fun mixing your own sandwich fillings. Here's one that is perfect for a picnic sandwich, or for spreading on a cracker.

You will need:

1 small tin of sweetcorn
1 small tin of tuna fish
4 slices of cucumber
3 tablespoons of mayonnaise or yoghurt
Raisins
2 teaspoons of lemon juice
Salt and pepper

What to do:

Open the tins with a tin opener and carefully pour away the juice.
Put the tuna and sweetcorn into a large bowl.
Chop up the cucumber slices into little squares and add these to the bowl.
Put in a tablespoon of raisins and add everything else on your list.

Mix it all up, and spread it on bread or crackers for a fresh summery treat.

 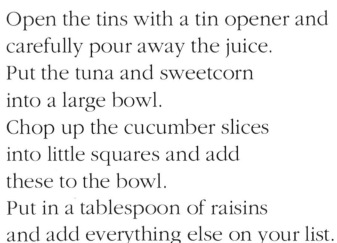

Picnic Pittas

Pitta breads are used a lot in Greece and Turkey. They look like bread pancakes, and you can make them into sandwich bags, just right for a packed lunch.

You will need:

Pitta breads
Butter or margarine
Lettuce leaves
1 cucumber
1 tomato
Slices of cold meat (ham, chicken or beef)
Slices of cheese
Mayonnaise or pickle

What to do:

Put the pitta bread on a chopping board and cut it in half.
Open out each half with your fingers to make a little bag.
Spread the insides with butter or margarine.
Slice the cucumber and tomato with a sharp knife (get a grown-up to help).
Stuff the pitta bread with a mixture of things from your list.

13

Tropical Salad

Here is a fruity salad that will add a sparkle to a picnic.

You will need:

½ a lettuce
4 slices of ham
2 bananas
2 teaspoons of lemon juice
2 fresh or tinned apricots
150ml of single cream
1 teaspoon of caster sugar
½ teaspoon of salt
1 pinch of pepper

What to do:

Tear the lettuce into small strips.
Chop the ham into small pieces (ask an adult to help).
Peel and slice the bananas.
Carefully cut the apricots in half. Remove the stones and chop the apricots into small squares.
Put everything into a mixing bowl and stir it up well. For a picnic, put the salad into a plastic bowl with a lid. Remember to take spoons and forks with you.

Lettuce Parcels

This is a very simple snack to make for your lunchbox. It makes a nice change from sandwiches.

You will need:

1 lettuce
Your favourite fillings (sardines, ham or cheese)
Cocktail sticks

What to do:

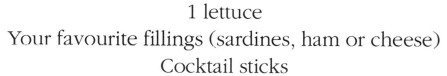

Remove the wrinkly outside lettuce leaves (they make good rabbit food).
Wash and dry the rest of the lettuce.
Break off some big leaves and put a filling on top.
Roll up the lettuce leaf into a little parcel.
Push a cocktail stick through it so that it doesn't unroll.

Try making several different sorts and surprise yourself at lunch time.

3 Sweet Things

Here's how to make some delicious sweet things. Don't eat too many though! You could also decorate small boxes with ribbons and put some sweets and biscuits inside. They make lovely presents for your friends and family.

Chocolate Truffles

These look very special and make smashing presents that cost almost nothing.

You will need:

100g of soft butter or soft cheese
2 tablespoons of icing sugar
6 tablespoons of drinking chocolate powder
Chocolate vermicelli

What to do:

Put the butter or cheese, icing sugar
and chocolate powder into a bowl.
Mix it all well with a wooden spoon.
Break off small pieces and roll them into balls.
Sprinkle the chocolate vermicelli over the balls.

Remember to clean your teeth after eating them!

Frosted Fruit

Here's a way to make fruit look really special and taste
wonderful too.

You will need:

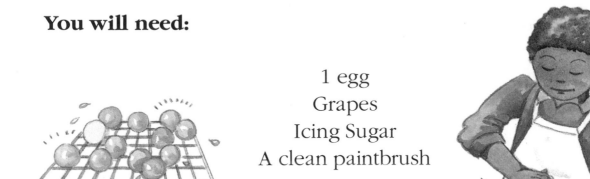

1 egg
Grapes
Icing Sugar
A clean paintbrush

What to do:

Crack the egg on to a saucer.
Put a glass over the yolk and tip the egg white into a bowl.
Whisk up the egg white with a fork or whisk until it is frothy.
Wash the grapes and put them on a wire rack.
Paint them with the egg white.
Dip them into a cup of icing sugar to coat them.
Put them back on the wire rack to dry.

Try using other fruit such as tangerine pieces or strawberries.

Muesli Chew Bars

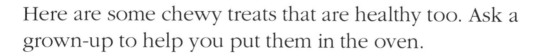

Here are some chewy treats that are healthy too. Ask a grown-up to help you put them in the oven.

You will need:

50g of dried apricots
50g of dates
50g of figs
50g of sultanas
50g of sunflower seeds
50g of hazelnuts
110g of porridge oats
2 tablespoons of concentrated apple juice

What to do:

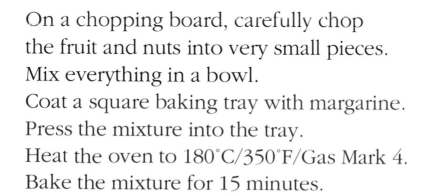

On a chopping board, carefully chop
the fruit and nuts into very small pieces.
Mix everything in a bowl.
Coat a square baking tray with margarine.
Press the mixture into the tray.
Heat the oven to 180°C/350°F/Gas Mark 4.
Bake the mixture for 15 minutes.
Cut it into slices.

These are great for lunchbox treats as well.

Banana Split

This was always my favourite pudding!

You will need:

4 large bananas
125g of raspberries or strawberries
3 tablespoons of icing sugar
150ml of whipping cream
4 scoops of ice cream

What to do:

Using a wooden spoon, press the raspberries
or strawberries through a sieve into a bowl.
Add the icing sugar.
Beat it all together with a fork to make a sauce.
Put the cream into a bowl and whisk it until it is thick.
Peel the bananas and put them on four plates.
Place a scoop of ice cream next to the bananas.
Cover the bananas with the sauce.
Add big dollops of cream at each end.

Call your friends and tuck in!

Rock and Roll Cakes

Try these tasty cakes on your friends. They are called rock cakes because they look all lumpy like little rocks.

You will need:

225g of self-raising flour
100g of sugar
100g of margarine
150g of mixed dried fruit
1 egg
4 tablespoons of milk
1 teaspoon of mixed spice

What to do:

Put the flour in a mixing bowl.
Cut the margarine into small lumps. Rub them into the flour with your fingertips until the mixture looks like breadcrumbs.
Mix in the egg, spice, sugar, fruit and milk.
Add more milk if the mixture is too dry.
Rub a little margarine on to a baking tray.
Put dollops of the mixture on the tray. The cakes will spread when cooking, so leave plenty of room for each one.
Ask a grown-up to help you bake them in the oven for 10–15 minutes at 220°C/450°F/Gas Mark 7.

Foolish Fruit

You can make a fruit fool with any soft fruit that you can mash up. This one is a strawberry fool.

You will need:

A small tub of strawberries
A large tub of plain yoghurt
25g of caster sugar
Fruit and wafers

What to do:

Put the strawberries in a bowl and mash them up with a fork.
Whisk the yoghurt in another bowl and add it to the strawberries.
Stir in the sugar.
Serve the fool into bowls and decorate each one with fruit and wafers.

You could try making faces with the decorations!

4 Party Food

Parties are lots of fun, and the food you eat should be fun too. These small nibbles are sure to go down well. Try adding extra things like nuts or lumps of cheese to make these snacks even more mouthwatering.

Marzipan Monsters

Use your imagination to make a plateful of tasty monsters.

You will need:

1 500g packet of marzipan
Natural food colourings
Raisins
1 stick of licorice
A clean paintbrush

What to do:

Squeeze the marzipan with your hands until it is soft.
Break off a piece and roll it into a ball, for the head.
Use a larger piece for the body.
Roll out some sausage shapes to make arms and legs (monsters can have as many as you like!)
Push in raisins for the eyes, nose and mouth.
Cut up the licorice to make horns.
Paint the monster with food colourings.
You can try lots of different shapes and sizes.
After all, who knows what a monster looks like?

Stuffed Dates

You will need:

1 packet of dates
50g of marzipan
Raisins or currants

What to do:

Carefully slit open the dates with a knife.
Remove the stones with your fingers.
Knead the marzipan until it is soft.
Roll out little sausage shapes and stuff each date.
Push some currants or raisins into the marzipan.

You could also try colouring the marzipan with natural red food colouring.
Then the dates would look like squashed insects!
Cream cheese is also tasty instead of marzipan.

Party Dips

Making party dips is great fun and so is eating them! They are perfect for sharing with friends.

Egg Mayonnaise Dip

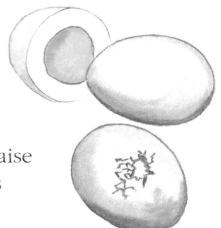

You will need:

1 small jar of mayonnaise
4 hard-boiled eggs

What to do:

Chop up the hard-boiled eggs into very small pieces. Put the mayonnaise into a serving bowl and stir in the chopped eggs.

Tomato Dip

You will need:

250g of cream cheese
6 tablespoons of tomato ketchup

What to do:

Put the cream cheese
into a serving bowl.
Add the tomato ketchup and
stir it all up well with a spoon.

How to eat dips:

Cut up little sticks of raw vegetables such as celery and carrot.
Arrange them on plates around the dips.
Then everyone dips a stick into the dip and chomps the lot.
Make sure you have plenty of tissues around.
Sometimes this gets a little bit messy!

Cocktail Snacks

These are little bite-size snacks stuck on cocktail sticks.
What you stick on is really up to you but how about trying this?

You will need:

1 small tin of pineapple chunks
150g of cheddar cheese
Stoned olives
4 slices of ham
Cocktail sticks

What to do:

Cut the cheese into small squares on a chopping board.
Roll up the ham slices and cut them into small segments.
Open the tin of pineapple with a tin opener and drain off
the juice.
Push a cocktail stick through an olive, a cheese square,
a pineapple chunk and a piece of ham.
Serve on a plate with the cocktail sticks pointing up in the air.

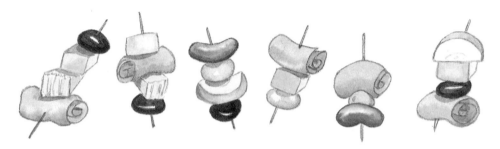

Try using other things such as pieces of sausage, apple or grapes.

Potatoes in their Jackets

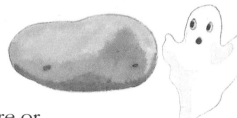

This is always a favourite especially at a bonfire or
Hallowe'en party.

You will need:

Large potatoes (enough for each of your friends)
Cheese
Butter or margarine

What to do:

Wash and dry the potatoes.
Prick them all over with a fork.
Put them on a baking tray so that they do not touch.
Ask a grown-up to help you bake them in an oven
for 1½–2 hours at 180°C/350°F/Gas Mark 4.
When they are cooked slit them open. Don't burn your fingers!
Put a knob of butter into each one and
grate cheese over the potato.
Add salt and pepper if you want to.

All sorts of fillings can be used in baked potatoes. What is
your favourite?

5 Drinks

After eating all the recipes in this book you might feel a bit thirsty. Here are some recipes for tasty drinks to wash it all down.

Banana Milkshake

You will need:

> 1 ripe banana
> 300ml of milk
> 4 tablespoons of vanilla ice cream

What to do:

Peel the banana and mash it with a fork in a bowl.
Put it into a tall jug and add the ice cream and milk.
Whisk it up until it is frothy using a hand whisk.
This might make your arm ache!
Pour the drink into two glasses.
When you taste it you will think
the hard work was worth it!

Strawberry Surprise

You will need:

> 300ml of natural yoghurt
> 150ml of milk
> 150ml of fizzy mineral water
> 8 large strawberries

What to do:

Pour the milk and yoghurt into a jug and whisk it until it is frothy.
With a fork, mash the strawberries in a bowl and add them to the jug.
Mix it well with a spoon and then half fill two glasses with the mixture.
Top up the glasses with fizzy mineral water.
Watch out though! It might whoosh over the top.

Soda Pop

You will need:

Vanilla ice cream
Fizzy lemonade or cola

What to do:

Put a scoop of ice cream
into a tall glass.
Top it up with lemonade or cola.
Drink it through a straw and
pretend you are on holiday.